MW00795411

Royal
Horticultural
Society

birthday BOOK

FRANCES
LINCOLN

NAME:
....
ADDRESS:
....
....
HOME NUMBER:
....
WORK NUMBER:
....
MOBILE NUMBER:
....
EMAIL ADDRESS:
....

introduction

Birthdays and anniversaries are never easy to remember. The *RHS Birthday Book* is the place to keep all your important dates together so that you will never have to suffer the embarrassment of forgetting them again.

The *RHS Birthday Book* showcases work held in the world-famous RHS Lindley Library. These include illustrations by Pieter Holsteyn the younger, born in Haarlem around 1614, Pierre-Joseph Redouté (1759–1840), Willliam Hooker (1779–1832), Lydia Penrose (1787–1842), Caroline Maria Applebee, whose earliest drawings are dated 1808 and the last 1852, Lilian Snelling (1879–1972), Cynthia Newsome-Taylor (1906–1983) and Graham Stuart Thomas (1909–2003).

01

january

02

03

04

05

january

06

07

08

09

january

10

11

12

13

january

14

15

16

17

january

18

19

20

21

january

22

23

24

25

january

26

27

28

29

january-february

30

31

01

02

february

03

04

05

06

february

07

08

09

10

february

11

12

13

14

february

15

16

17

18

february

19

20

21

22

february

23

24

25

26

february

27

28

29

01

march

02

03

04

05

march

06

07

08

09

march

10

11

12

13

march

14

15

16

17

march

18

19

20

21   *march*

22

23

24

25

march

26

27

28

29

march-april

30

31

01

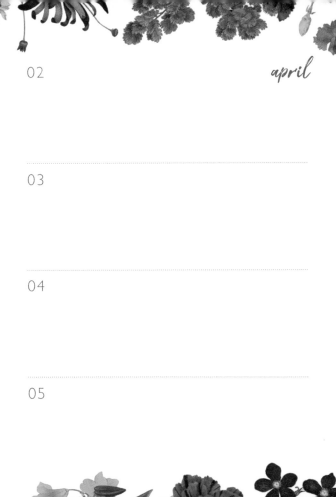

02

april

03

04

05

06

april

07

08

09

10

april

11

12

13

14

april

15

16

17

18

april

19

20

21

22

april

23

24

25

26

april

27

28

29

april-may

01

02

03

04

may

05

06

07

08

may

09

10

11

12

may

13

14

15

16

may

17

18

19

20

may

21

22

23

24

may

25

26

27

28

may

29

30

31

01

june

02

03

04

05

june

06

07

08

09

june

10

11

12

13

june

14

15

16

17

june

18

19

20

21   *june*

22

23

24

25

june

26

27

28

29

june-july

30

01

02

03

july

04

05

06

07

july

08

09

10

11

july

12

13

14

15

july

16

17

18

19

july

20

21

22

23

july

24

25

26

27

july

28

29

30

31

july-august

01

02

03

04

august

05

06

07

08

august

09

10

11

12

august

13

14

15

16

august

17

18

19

20

august

21

22

23

24

august

25

26

27

28

august

29

30

31

01

September

02

03

04

05

September

06

07

08

09

September

10

11

12

13

September

14

15

16

17

September

18

19

20

21

September

22

23

24

25

September

26

27

28

29

September-october

30

01

02

03

october

04

05

06

07

october

08

09

10

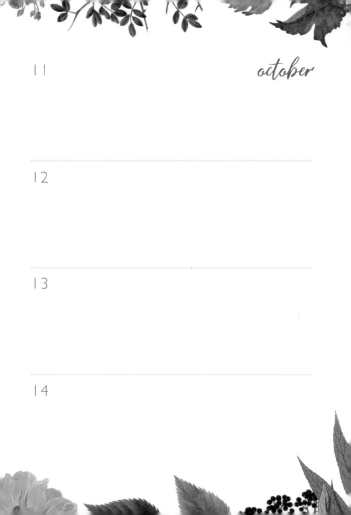

11

october

12

13

14

15

october

16

17

18

19

october

20

21

22

23

october

24

25

26

27

october

28

29

30

31

october-november

01

02

03

04

november

05

06

07

08

november

09

10

11

12

november

13

14

15

16

november

17

18

19

20

november

21

22

23

24

november

25

26

27

28

november-december

29

30

01

02

december

03

04

05

06

december

07

08

09

10

december

11

12

13

14

december

15

16

17

18

december

19

20

21

22

23

24

25

26

december

27

28

29

30

december

31

The Royal Horticultural Society Birthday Book

Copyright © Quarto Publishing plc 2018

Illustrations are from the RHS Lindley Library copyright
© the Royal Horticultural Society 2018
and printed under licence granted by the Royal Horticultural
Society, Registered Charity number 222879/SC038262.

An interest in gardening is all you need to
enjoy being a member of the RHS.
For more information visit our website rhs.org.uk

First published in 2018 by Frances Lincoln, an imprint of
The Quarto Group. www.QuartoKnows.com

Cover & interior design by Sarah Allberrey

ISBN: 978-0-7112-3946-3

Printed in Singapore
15 14 13 12 11 10